THE FINAL
YEARS OF FIRST
NORTHAMPTON

MATT COOPER

AMBERLEY

First published 2021

Amberley Publishing
The Hill, Stroud
Gloucestershire, GL5 4EP

www.amberley-books.com

Copyright © Matt Cooper, 2021

The right of Matt Cooper to be identified as
the Author of this work has been asserted in
accordance with the Copyrights, Designs and
Patents Act 1988.

ISBN 978 1 3981 0782 3 (print)
ISBN 978 1 3981 0783 0 (ebook)

British Library Cataloguing in Publication Data.
A catalogue record for this book is available from
the British Library.

Typesetting by SJmagic DESIGN SERVICES, India.
Printed in Great Britain.

Introduction

First Northampton was the last incarnation of Northampton Transport, a title given by First Group in 1998. However, the company can trace its origins back to 1881. Northampton Street Tramways began services that year with horse-drawn vehicles and trams, their stables located off Abington Street in the heart of the town centre. In 1901 the operation was bought by the council, becoming 'Northampton Corporation Tramways', and a new depot was established at St James for the electric trams then in use. Motor buses were introduced and would see off the trams by 1934. Over time Northampton Corporation Transport built up a standardised fleet with the favoured type being a combination of Daimler chassis and Roe bodywork. Vehicles were smartly presented in a red and white livery, which continued into the 'OMO', or driver-only, era. In 1968 Northampton received the last rear-entrance bus built for the home market and crew operation in the town would continue until 1985.

Deregulation in 1986 didn't significantly change the organisation. To comply with the 1985 Transport Act a separate legal identity was established and the company was renamed 'Northampton Transport Ltd'. All Saints Church replaced the town crest as the logo. The agency agreement between Northampton Transport and United Counties largely continued but under what might be termed a gentleman's agreement. This kept each operator to their own areas of the town; joint services were still operated and revenue shared.

Historically Northampton is famed for its shoe and boot industry, which greatly expanded the town and put it on the map. This industry still continues today, albeit on a much smaller scale. Designated a planned new town in 1965, Northampton would see considerable development from this point onwards, especially in the eastern and southern districts. Industry and employment shifted towards warehousing, distribution, finance and administrative roles. Edge-of-town industrial parks grew from this shift. Joining these outlying areas in the mid-1990s was one of Northampton's most significant employers. The higher education establishment Nene College developed over two campus sites to eventually gain university status in 2005. The provision of transport was required, which is detailed in the book. Around the turn of the millennium the process of regentrification occurred and the town centre benefitted from new leisure, retail and residential developments.

Mention must be given to Greyfriars bus station, which opened in 1976. The massive concrete structure gained media attention in later life as one of the UK's most hideous buildings. Prior to its existence Corporation buses had used town centre streets as their terminus. Out-of-town United Counties services utilised Derngate bus station, while private coach operators had parking facilities at the Mayorhold. The new building allowed everything to be centralised. Never truly fulfilling its intended purpose as office space as well as a bus station, continual decline ensued. Though gloomy, it was roomy – buses had space at their allocated bays, while passengers enjoyed indoor accommodation and quick access via underpasses to shops and local streets. Greyfriars bus station outlived First Northampton by only six months, closing in March 2014, and being quite dramatically brought down by controlled explosion a year later. The site has yet to be rejuvenated.

Northampton Transport's shrewd accounting paid off and the delivery of six new buses per year continued right up until 1993. The organisation was also rewarded in the financial year 1991/2, being ranked top as Britain's most profitable bus company. Pre-tax profit to turnover had reached 19.4 per cent, but by 1993 the council expressed an interest in selling Northampton Transport to raise funds for other projects. Following a short but intense period of competition with United Counties, Grampian Regional Transport (GRT) bought the operation on 14 October 1993. At the point of purchase the majority of the company's operations were within the Northampton Borough, an area of approximately thirty square miles. Some private hire and coach work continued. It is here, just over a century into Northampton Transport's history, that we join what was to be the last twenty years of operation. The company ran its last bus on 14 September 2013.

GRT inherited a well-kept standardised fleet comprising mainly double-deckers. Numbering thirty, the newest and most common was the Alexander RV-bodied Volvo Citybus. Each carried a locally associated name and were what might be considered the last standard 'Corporation' bus. In 1987 Northampton Transport had experimented with a small batch of minibuses, some of which remained upon takeover. Now part of a larger concern, the opportunity to transfer these out along with another unpopular type, the East Lancs-bodied Leyland Olympians, was hastily pursued. In November 1993 GRT also acquired neighbouring county municipal operator Leicester Citybus. A common livery was devised based on Grampian's own style and vehicles of both undertakings quickly received their new colours.

In 1993 the UK had launched its first low-floor buses in Merseyside. The following year trial batches for London were in service. Northampton Transport received three Alexander Ultra Volvo B10Ls in late 1995, still making them one of the first twenty operators to launch low-floor vehicles. This shows how slow the UK was in adopting this type of vehicle, as European operators were widely using low-floor buses at this time.

GRT's sole ownership was relatively short-lived as by April 1995 a merger with the Badgerline Group would form First Bus. A year later Northampton Transport would see changes on an unprecedented scale as the network, vehicles types, and liveries became unrecognisable from Corporation Transport days. First would operate in five of Northamptonshire's neighbouring counties, as well as expand within the home county and borough. School, college, university and works contracts along with a number of services set up with help of the 'Rural Bus Grant' would be won. Having a fleet of low-floor vehicles already in place helped win some of the new work that specified this type of bus, one extreme example being the Sunday-only 442 service running from Gretton to Corby! This rapid expansion was initially to the detriment of the core town services, some of which were established as 'quality corridor' schemes. However, staffing and vehicle availability were causing the company major problems. These were addressed relatively quickly with a lot of the tendered work surrendered by 1999, thus enabling public confidence to be largely restored. Such is the cyclical nature of staffing levels that by 2000 Northampton were in a position to loan drivers to Leicester on a regular basis.

Now named First Group, significant service alterations in April 2001 and 2002 brought about the start of what seemed like almost constant change. The traditional routes, many originating during Corporation days, were altered with most becoming cross-town services. Regular Sunday work began, though traditionally such services were contracted out to Stagecoach United Counties. As with other First Group Companies the network was branded under the 'Overground' banner with routes receiving colour coding. This was seldom referred to by staff or the public but looked distinctive on the network map and the newly received Wright Eclipse-bodied Volvo B7s smartly carried their branding.

The regional division within which Northampton sat with First also changed over the years. Initially just tied with Leicester, by 1999 the division also included the East Anglian and Essex operations. This would change and by mid-2002 the First Midlands division contained Leicester, Northampton and what was once Midland Red West. With each change came different policies, ideas and methods of working. Cost savings could be made by centralising operations, which is obviously appealing and had already occurred within the engineering department. However a feeling of loss of local control and knowledge was experienced, especially with regard to scheduling. At this time very few operators had a web presence and mobile phone technology was still relatively primitive. Service information was obtained face-to-face or by means of a telephone or even postal enquiry. With a considerable number of passengers using Greyfriars bus station as an end destination or interchange, the decision to close the ticket office and enquiry point at this location in January 2003 was rather surprising. Each of the two members of staff working there could answer the majority of quick queries the public had. The face of First thus became a leaflet rack and sign displaying the depot telephone number.

Things were much more positive by 2005. With schools and contract services consolidated and unreliable cross-town routes eliminated, an impressive route network was being operated. Fourteen high-frequency town services were in the hands of a fleet of nineteen brand new Wright-bodied Volvo B7TL double-deck and Volvo B7RLE single-deck vehicles. Joining twenty-five similar '02' plate vehicles, together these buses made up an impressive fleet. Only a handful of contracts and rural services were being operated at this time, giving maximum focus on the town network.

Sadly this wasn't to last and as early as 2006 the Volvos were being replaced with older step-entrance vehicles, some of which Northampton Transport had withdrawn with the introduction of the new low-floor buses! Routes operated jointly with Stagecoach United Counties were stopped back in 2002. However, leading up to 2005 a number of routes operated by First ran in competition over large patches of Stagecoach's territory. These would be cut back and with Stagecoach introducing a large number of new easy-access vehicles First's image was beginning to look tired. The network map dated 2010 paints a sad picture. Only eight routes exist, with just one heading out to the lucrative eastern district. Stagecoach was by now operating over the unhighlighted areas, offering a good town network.

Other operations running from St James depot at this time included a yellow school bus division and National Express contracts. The latter ran under the leadership of First Wessex in a separate office between 2003 and 2007, when the routes were lost to Arriva Midlands. Trialling a yellow school bus in 2000, it would be four years until the concept was introduced on routes for Northampton School for Girls. Four vehicles were operated that transferred within First when Northampton depot closed and the contracts passed to local coach operators using more conventional vehicles.

First Group had been disposing of parts of its UK bus operation from 2011. These included all London depots, Bracknell, Redditch, Kidderminster, Chester and Wigan. Having strongly denied that Northampton was on the list, by July 2013 the announcement was made and operations were wound down route by route. In most cases Stagecoach Midlands (as it was known by then) was registering each one by one. Uno, which was operating routes centring on the university, would also benefit from First's contraction. In August 2013 just thirteen vehicles were operated, including the Luton Airport to Luton Parkway station shuttle for First Capital Connect. This operation would later transfer to First Essex at Chelmsford. This compares to ninety-one vehicles being used at the height of recent operations in 1998. Saturday 14 September 2013 was the final day of operation and red route 2 the final service. Passengers on the last night were able to travel back to the depot in the former Eastern Counties Wright-bodied Scania and watch the door be unceremoniously closed on 132 years of Northampton transport history.

Many differing areas of operation, liveries and vehicle types used by First Northampton are featured in this book, though they couldn't all be included. In 2002 eight different chassis and seventeen body types were in use! A nightmare for the engineering department and driving staff familiarising themselves with the types. Even the vehicles fleet numbers changed several times during this period, many of which are detailed.

My grateful thanks are due for the photographic assistance of David Pike, David Henderson, Raymond Bedford and Nigel Wheeler, who filled in some essential gaps. Also to Carl Thomas of Pindar Creative for permission to use the 2001 and 2010 network maps. These will show just how much the operation contracted over those nine years and give the geographical layout of the town and its suburbs. Bob Jackson for the proofreading and advice, and to Connor Stait and staff at Amberley Publishing for taking on the project. Most importantly I am indebted my wife and family for their support, help, understanding and patience throughout this book's creation.

First Northampton network map from April 2001. This followed some significant changes and the majority of the routes were cross-town. Some of the colour coding used would be applied to routes a year later with the Overground launch. The only one applied at this time was Red for new route 2.

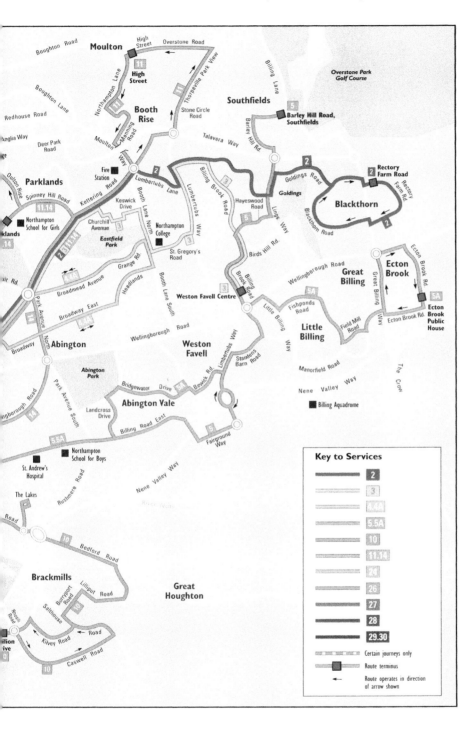

Key to Services

▬▬▬▬	2
▬▬▬▬	3
▬▬▬▬	14A
▬▬▬▬	5.5A
▬▬▬▬	10
▬▬▬▬	11.14
▬▬▬▬	24
▬▬▬▬	26
▬▬▬▬	27
▬▬▬▬	28
▬▬▬▬	29.30

▬▬▬ Certain journeys only

■ Route terminus

← Route operates in direction of arrow shown

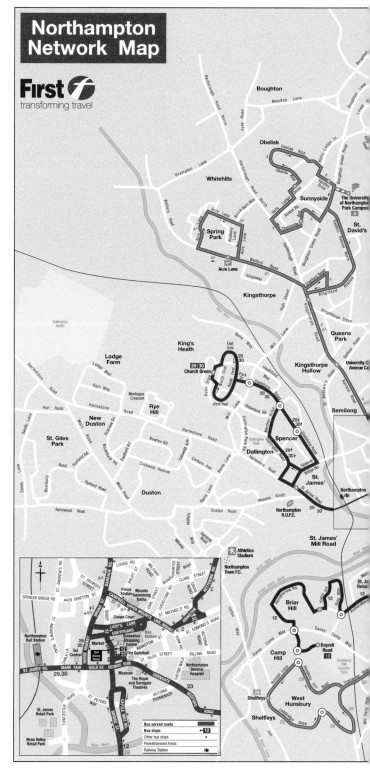

By comparison the September 2010 view is more useful as a map of the town with just eight routes remaining.

2		28	
4 4A		29 30	
12			
Other First in Northampton services			
23			
Route terminus			2
Bus runs in direction of arrow			→
Railway line and station			
Timing Point			○

Produced by FWT 29.9.10 www.fwt.co.uk

NT to First, via GRT with coats of many colours

The last of the 'red bus' era on Kettering Road, February 1993. 74 (ABD 74X), one of the last of the Bristol VRs to be delivered, is overtaken by Alexander-bodied Volvo Citybus 85 (F85 XBD), one of the first of this type. A batch of six Leyland Olympians sat awkwardly in between and was quickly dispensed with under GRT ownership. Both vehicles look resplendent in the last version of the red and cream livery, 85 sporting the local name scroll *Richard the Lionheart*. A matter of months after this image was taken a lot was about to change. (David Henderson)

Part of the penultimate batch of six Alexander RV-bodied Volvo Citybuses, 124 (K124 URP) carried local name *The Welsh House*. Seen on Ring Way, Briar Hill by the Double Four pub (that has since been replaced by housing) it is working established cross-town route 26 towards Holly Lodge Drive, Kingsthorpe in August 1993. This was during the 'bus war' with Stagecoach after the council had expressed a wish to sell Northampton Transport. Stagecoach ran the 85 between Briar Hill and the town centre, which can be seen to the top right of the picture. So too can part of Greyfriars bus station to the right of the pub's sign. (David Pike)

What could be considered the last Corporation bus, Volvo Citybus 132 (K132 GNH) had only just been delivered to St James Depot in this July 1993 shot. Originally intended to carry 'L' prefix registrations, the final batch of six were pressed into early use due to increased competition from Stagecoach. The bus would see further service through First Group in Glasgow. (Nigel Wheeler)

Northampton Transport's standard double-decker of the late 1970s was the Bristol VR with Alexander AL bodywork, thirty-five being delivered during 1977/8. The upper deck was uniquely styled for Northampton with a peaked front dome and curved rear. Dual-door specification was standard at the time. Six were replaced annually from 1989 but privatisation in 1993 kept nine of this type in service until 1999. Seen at St Giles Square in May 1996 is 54 (CNH 54T), wearing full GRT colours and local advertising for Oliver Adams the bakers. The Guildhall's eastern extension, seen behind the bus, opened in 1991 and superbly compliments the main adjoining building which dates from 1864. (David Pike)

The last vehicle into GRT livery was 74 (ABD 74X). By this time the company was under FirstBus ownership and the 'rose and thistle' were missing from the fleet name. 'Welcome to FirstBus' stickers were applied to the front nearside and rear windows when the organisation was initially created. In this view 74 is turning from George Row into Drapery on 7 July 1997.

On 7 July 1997 94 (H294 VRP) departing Greyfriars bus station was one of only two Volvo Citybuses to feature a dot matrix destination screen. Despite being one of the most centrally located towns in England, Northampton boasts an area called Headlands served by long-standing circular Corporation routes 4 and 5. The glass-covered footbridge over Lady's Lane to the left of the picture provided access to the mass of office space that sat above the bus station.

The original livery applied to Northampton and Leicester vehicles from February 1997 under First Bus ownership was this red and cream style. Favouring Northampton, the maroon band is the only Leicester-inspired feature. Local name scroll *Delapre Abbey* had been reapplied. The first three Volvo Citybuses were painted at Northampton with the majority so treated at Leicester. 89 (H289 VRP) is working route 20 along Billing Road East on 11 April 1997. (David Pike)

Also keeping its local name scroll, *Rushmills Penny Black* was 90 (H290 VRP) showing local 'Northampton Transport' fleet names. Here it is turning from Drapery into Mercers Row on 7 July 1997.

A red band was added around the middle of the vehicles, giving a better appearance. This became the 'standard' NT/LCB livery. With 'First' names more prominent localism could still exist, as shown by the smaller 'Northampton' lettering on the side of 122 (WSU 481, K122 URP). This Volvo Citybus was rebodied by East Lancs in 1998 following an accident. Seen at John Dryden House council offices working the lunchtime shuttle on 24 February 2000.

Previously numbered 743, Wright Eclipse-bodied Volvo B7L 340 (MV02 VBA) shows First Group standard low-floor livery with 'Overground' branding. Unconnected with the London surface rail network, Bristol Omnibus had pioneered the 'Overground' brand including tube-style map and colour-coded routes. The format was inherited under Badgerline and used by First. Northampton gained its 'Overground' in September 2002 with the B7L vehicles being branded in December. The camera caught 340 carrying orange branding for route 27 at Mereway Tesco on 25 January 2003.

A corporate image was sought by First for all non-low-floor vehicles. Volvo Citybus 294 (H294 VRP) shows the blank canvas to which a vinyl magenta fade-out band would be applied above the blue skirt. However, many vehicles ran in this unfinished state for some months. Seen at Hunsbury Hill Road on 21 April 2001, this was to be the last day of route 26.

The magenta fade-out is shown on former Leicester Dennis Falcon 625 (L625 XFP), nicknamed 'Barbie 2. Looking smart when initially applied, any repairs to the vinyl side panels made for a rather patchy appearance, as if plasters had been added! One of six transferred from Leicester, 625 is operating route 3 at Rectory Farm Road, the eastern side of the cross-town route on 23 August 2002. A member of the last batch of Dennis Falcons to be built, this was the penultimate example.

Experimental liveries before FG2 were tried at Leicester and Northampton including one of white, green and yellow, and this red and blue scheme. This was carried on both ex-Great Yarmouth Volvo Citybuses bringing 'red' back to Northampton. None of the schemes were adopted and corporatism won the day! 280 (E40 OAH) operates route 69 at Ecton Brook Road on 22 April 2000.

St James Depot

Extensions and modifications to St James Depot over the years can be seen in this view from 30 December 2001. This was a Sunday and at this time no services were operated by First in the town, a throwback to the days of council ownership. Scania 359 (S359 MFP) is about to leave for Market Harborough to work rail replacement duties on behalf of Midland Mainline. Being kept undercover, no de-icing was required in these wintry conditions.

The oldest part of St James Depot sits adjacent to Sharman Road. This was constructed in the early 1900s and was intended for trams. The iron roads would only see around thirty years use, with the last tram running in the town on 15 December 1934. This part of the depot became the workshop area and the tramlines were (and still are) in situ. 30 December 2001 saw four of the six pits in use with vehicles 41, 294, 267 and 132 awaiting mechanical attention. The former paint shop is to the right in the distance.

In July 1993 Volvo Citybus 102 (D102 XNV) is jacked up and receiving some attention at the rear of the workshops. Still to coach specification, which included upper-deck wipers, 102's paintwork shines in the natural light provided by part of the large glass roof. All manner of skilled tradesmen worked at the site in the past and an extensive stock of spare parts was kept. Most were gone by late 1997 when rationalisation saw Leicester perform the majority of engineering tasks with parts being ordered in as required. (Nigel Wheeler)

The main body of the garage built in 1939, which measured 260 feet long by 90 feet wide, was effectively another extension to the existing building. With only three central support pillars (one can be seen behind the bus) the depot was very open, which made manoeuvring vehicles that bit easier. Newly delivered Volvo B7L 714 (later 355) (MV02 VCP) is seen on the cleaners' bay on 20 August 2002.

Seventy-five Wright Eclipse-bodied Volvo B7Ls were new to First Manchester in 2002. These were used on Commonwealth Games contracts and dispersed to other fleets once that operation was complete. Northampton received twenty-five of these between August and October that year, and they originally ran with their Manchester fleet numbers. First to arrive was 714 (MV02 VCP), seen on 20 August 2002 still displaying the Commonwealth Games vinyl.

Heading to the rear of the depot building and back to July 1993, East Lancs-bodied Leyland Olympian 78 (A78 RRP) awaits its next turn of duty. One of a batch of six similar vehicles new in 1984 they were rather unloved at Northampton and under Grampian ownership were quickly transferred north to Aberdeen in 1994. Numerous outbuildings can be seen behind the bus, most rented out to other companies for varying uses. Over a period of time each would be demolished and the whole area eventually cleared prior to Church's, the shoe company, acquiring the site in 2013. (Nigel Wheeler)

In the back yard of St James Depot, there was a mix of overflow parking for the operational fleet and an area for those vehicles awaiting withdrawal. Lincoln Road ends at the boundary fence. The uneven ground was resurfaced a couple of years after this picture was taken. On Saturday 19 February 2000 ex-Lincoln Bristol VR 46 (UFW 40W) enjoys a day off from its school contract work. Native Northampton Alexander-bodied 52 (CNH 52T), which had last been used in Leicester, awaits its fate.

Northampton inherited eleven Metrobuses all used by Leicester, six originating with Midland Bluebird. The latter had their Scottish Bus Group destination boxes replaced with the layout as depicted. 34 (AUT 34Y), new to Leicester, and 266 (ULS 642X) have completed their week's work on 29 December 2001 and rest for the weekend. They are overlooked by Northampton's 'lighthouse', a 127-metre structure completed in 1982 for Express Lifts, who used it as a testing facility. Perhaps the Headlands term wasn't so out of place after all!

Duple-bodied Leyland Tiger 410 (EWR 653Y) was one of four such vehicles acquired from Eastern National having been delivered new to West Yorkshire PTE. 410 retained its coach seats and gave a comfortable ride for passengers, although the high steps weren't too practical on town work. Captured at the rear of St James Depot on 27 April 2000, the vehicle was withdrawn a week later.

Former London Buses Ltd 'H' class Dennis Dominator B103 WUW, numbered 142 at Northampton, was one of a pair acquired from First Capital, whose London-style destination box carried an adapted Leicester blind. On 29 December 2001 it is sitting among a trio of former Aberdeen Atlanteans, all displaying various school bus route numbers but not required for duties over the Christmas holiday period.

With a Northern Counties family likeness, two years separate Dennis Dominator 141 (B102 WUW), new to London Regional Transport as H2, and Leyland Atlantean 6479 (ANA 629Y), new to Greater Manchester PTE as 4629. By 3 August 2002 141 has had a provincial-style destination screen fitted, unlike 142. It will be noted that 6479 retained its former Huddersfield fleet number while at Northampton. The Manchester-style body has no ticket machine facility, limiting its use (although not always!) to schools work.

In 2002 the whole area at the back of the depot was resurfaced, giving a much tidier appearance. A collection of vehicles await their afternoon duties on 28 November 2002, including East Lancs-bodied Dennis Dominator 148 (G667 FKA), new to North Western.

Almost all of the thirty Alexander-bodied Volvo Citybuses clocked up twenty years of service, 97–99 and 121/122 were always at Northampton and the remainder served at several other locations within the First Group empire. One that wasn't so lucky was 131 (K131 GNH), originally named *Rose of the Shires*. It was languishing in the corner of the rear yard at St James depot on 16 June 2003 after an arson attack to the top deck during mid-April of that year. The vehicle sat in this position for several months pending its future which, in the end, was the scrapyard.

Trainee drivers could learn in this very unusual Alexander TC-bodied Dennis Dorchester 911 (A205 UYS). New to Kelvin in 1984 and used by Greater Glasgow as CD95, the vehicle was acquired from Sheffield Mainline in 2000. Shared between Northampton and Leicester it is seen here at the back of St James Depot on 29 December 2001.

At the end of the wash road inside the depot we can see preserved Daimler CVG6 154 (ANH 154) and, on loan from Mainline, Volvo B10BLE 786 (R86 XHL). Fitted with a Northampton blind, the Sheffield via point 'rolling pin' can still be seen in the nearside windscreen. On 26 July 2002 the loan vehicle is about to depart for the PM peak bus working on route 29. The wear to the depot floor from vehicles turning out of the wash can be seen, as can part of an ornate circular window, which once formed part of the old depot wall before the 1939 extension.

Vehicles that 'ran in' during the day were lined up nose-in along this wall. Some received routine attention by engineering staff while others were cleaned or laid over until the evening peak. On 28 December 2002 Volvo B7L 344 (formally 713) (MV02 VCO) shows the Overground branding applied to 'purple line' vehicles on routes 29/30.

A logical step by Northamptonshire C.C. in 2006 was the launch of an all-operators ticket and brand for the Northampton Borough called 'Buzz Card'. The press launch was 23 January 2006 on the forecourt of St James Depot. Some of the newest vehicles were exhibited by Stagecoach (Dart 34772), First (Volvo B7RLE 66970) and MK Metro (Optare Solo 24), the latter company having acquired contract work in the town. Also in view is the former office and administration block behind the buses and part of the original tramway building. The two bricked-up arches would have been tram roads.

Greyfriars bus station

Volvo Citybus 97 (J297 GNV), the last with local name scroll reapplied (*William Carey 1761-1834*), is loading on bay 20 at Greyfriars bus station on 7 July 1997. Having natural light, this was one of the better bays and if drivers stopped short of the stand a swift departure could be made without reversing! An additional bonus was that if a toilet break was urgently required the staff facilities on the concourse were next to this bay! Apart from a period at Worcester, between August 2007 and October 2008, 97 spent its entire life at Northampton and was scrapped in late 2010.

Departing the eastern end of Greyfriars is East Lancs-bodied Volvo B10M 115 (J115 MRP), unique in the Northampton fleet. Showing the GRT livery as applied to single-deck vehicles, 115 is working route 25 to Kingsthorpe Nene College (now University of Northampton) on 7 March 1997. The former council offices of Northampton House, looming behind, are now flats.

With dual carriageway surrounding the former bus station, traffic flow was rarely compromised. On 1 May 1998 Wright Axcess-Ultralow-bodied Scania L113 342 (R342 SUT), of the original batch of this type for Northampton and Leicester, has departed at the eastern end and crossed to the nearside of Lady's Lane to make its way towards Kingsthorpe.

The Kings Heath routes 2 and 10 had been converted to super-low-floor with the arrival of three Wright-bodied Scanias. Also on 1 May 1998 the last of the trio, 343 (R343 SUT), loads on bay 20. Unusual was the use of roller destination blinds and electronic numbers, which somewhat resembled railway station clocks in use at that time!

Still wearing the colours of its previous owner Ipswich Buses, 629 (C109 SDX) displays an 'on hire' board despite by then being part of the fleet. The Dennis Falcon with dual-door Northern Counties body works north to south cross-town service 25, departing the western end of Greyfriars on 7 July 1997 and joining the road giving its name to the bus station.

The original routes worked by the six gas-powered Volvo B10Ls were cross-town 29/79 (Kingsthorpe Acre Lane–Town–Billing Road–Ecton Brook). On 27 May 1999, 504 (P504 MVV) has just departed Greyfriars and is heading to the northern end of the route.

At the same location on Lady's Lane, on 17 March 1998 we can see how well traffic could flow from the old bus station. First's former Timeline Alexander-bodied Leyland Tiger 407 (F37 ENF), substituting for a low-floor bus, leads the way. Following is one-time NT Bristol VR (VVV 61S) smartly turned out by owner Country Lion. A Stagecoach United Counties Volvo Olympian with Northern Counties body creeps out of Greyfriars behind.

The last Wright Eclipse-bodied Volvo B7L to arrive from Manchester was 348 (MV02 VBU), which on 23 September 2003 lays over on bay 20. The font of the branding differed from the rest of the batch (compare to the photo on page 23). The automatic sliding door fitted to this bay can be seen. Along with bays A & H this was a gas bus legacy, their services originally using these bays. The bus wash used by Stagecoach is behind the large red 'arrowed' wall.

Sitting in front of the wash on 20 March 1998 is Leicester Dennis Dominator 240 (FUT 240V) with East Lancs bodywork. This vehicle was on loan to Northampton when the picture was taken and would later become a driver training vehicle.

Once a body and chassis combination favoured by Leicester, when 240's days as a driver trainer were over the vehicle was sold for preservation, initially on the south coast but now back in home territory in the Midlands. Seen at the Provincial Society's Stokes Bay bus rally on 7 August 2011 in as-withdrawn condition.

Merry-go-round the town centre

Providing a useful and fast link from the Kingsthorpe area to the rail station and town centre was route 21. Volvo Citybus 96 (J296 GNV) unloads at the 'Castle Station' bus stop on 27 May 1997 in full GRT livery, complete with fleet names, local name scroll *Becketts Well* and the original white-on-black blinds. The railway station has since been redeveloped and buses can no longer easily access the station forecourt area. 96 was one of a number of the type that went on to work in Edinburgh.

The process of regentrification started in Northampton around the turn of the Millennium. Volvo Citybus 211 (D101 XNV), one of a pair of 1986 East Lancs-bodied coaches once numbered 1 and 2, were downgraded to bus work in the latter part of their lives. New leisure complex Sol Central is under construction on 30 September 2000 as 211 runs dead to the bus station. This bus would also finish its days in Edinburgh.

Formerly on the site of Barclaycard offices, Sol Central brought back a cinema and other leisure facilities to the town centre. 298 (J298 GNV), the last of the type to wear the red and cream livery, also makes its way to the bus station to take up its day's work on 1 March 2002. This bus spent its whole life in Northampton and was scrapped when the depot closed in 2013.

One of Northampton's most historic buildings, All Saints Church, was used as the NT logo between 1987 and privatisation in 1993. Volvo Citybus 84 (F84 XBD) passes in front of the church on route 8 on 6 August 1997. This was the second of the original 1989 batch, carrying the name *Northampton Castle* and showing the coach (lower) and dual-purpose (upper) seats fitted to this vehicle.

The bus stop at the top of Drapery was for many years used by cross-town route 26 to Kingsthorpe. During the 1960s the building used by Debenhams was inserted between two much-older structures. Trams would also have used this thoroughfare, their northerly destination also Kingsthorpe, where their passenger shelter still exists to this day. In more recent times on 7 July 1997 92 (H292 VRP), named *Master Cobbler*, waits for passengers.

At the south end after turning out of Drapery buses travelled in a clockwise direction around All Saints Church. Volvo Citybus 125 (K125 URP), named *Notre Dame*, makes the turn heading to Camp Hill on 30 September 2000. This vehicle passed to First Potteries after service with Northampton. Receiving a repaint and refurbishment with them, the vehicle was the final survivor of the thirty NT examples, lasting until September 2015.

In December 1999 Northampton received three Wright Axcess-Floline-bodied Scania L94s to replace earlier examples that were sent to Leicester following a depot fire at Abbey Park Road. First of the trio is 362 (V362 CNH), operating route 27 along Drapery on 30 September 2000. It is passing one of very few traditional tobacconists left in the area.

Heading into the town centre at Abington Square on 22 December 2001 is 292 (H292 VRP) in full 'FG2' livery with *Northampton* under the cab window. Still with original white-on-black roller blinds, the 4A ran from Headlands to Kingsthorpe. The public conveniences have since been converted into a retail outlet.

Almost at the location of its local name scroll, *Market Square*, which is adjacent to Drapery, 129 (K129 GNH) is part of the last batch of Alexander-bodied Volvo Citybuses delivered in 1993. There has been a market in Northampton since 1189 and on its present site since 1235. On 20 March 1998 the driver changes the blinds for his next journey.

In August 2000 four First Group standard Wright Axcess-Floline-bodied Scania L94s arrived from Yorkshire Rider (Bradford). Their main duties were on the quality corridor routes such as the 27, on which 365 (S101 CSG) is operating on 30 September 2000. The red bus stop flags and red bus shelters were common in the town from the mid-1990s as part of the 'facelift for public transport'.

The Alexander-AL bodied Bristol VRs were not registered in sequence due to long lead times during their construction. Numerically the last was 70 (VVV 70S), seen here on Billing Road by Northampton General Hospital complete with NT-style gold fleet numbers. Used as a driver trainer towards the end of its life, 70 was once considered a candidate for preservation. Sadly this never came to be and the bus was scrapped, the registration number bought by a driver and put on his car! (David Pike)

Four of these smart Duple 300-bodied Volvo B10Ms were operated on a variety of routes and, in their early days, on private hire work. Last of the batch, 114 (G114 ENV) awaits custom outside St Giles Street Post Office on 29 July 2000 on Saturdays-only Park and Ride route A to Cliftonville House. Two vehicles operated this route on a 10-minute frequency.

Only just over a mile from the town centre, this was the car park of the borough council offices, not used by them on Saturdays. Fellow vehicle 112 (G112 ENV) is seen on 28 June 2003. This was the last day of route A despite good loads being carried weekly. Northampton was thereafter left with no P&R facilities. 112 would shortly be operating the final 17.30 departure from St Giles Street.

Out and about, Northampton

Alexander-bodied MCW Metrobus 31 (AUT 31Y) was one of five from Leicester that worked all manner of routes at Northampton. On 20 May 2000 it is seen at Lumbertubs Lane heading east to Rectory Farm. Route 7 was scheduled to work with largely similar route 3 and provided links from the eastern district to Weston Favell Shopping Centre and the town centre.

Another type inherited from Leicester was the Dennis Dominator with bodywork by various manufacturers, in this case East Lancs. 79 (B79 MJF) carries the experimental red and blue livery, including a 'willow leaf' on each side usually denoting low-floor, which this vehicle certainly wasn't! Seen at Oulton Rise, Parklands, 79 is operating route 11 on 5 January 2002.

Volvo Citybus 100 (J210 GNV) is at Ecton Brook Road operating the advertised 'quick link to town' route 69 on 6 January 2000. Vehicles of the H and J registered batches up to 99 had registrations matching their fleet numbers, albeit preceeded by a 2 as the DVLA wanted to charge extra for a two-digit number series! Registrations containing 00 were even harder to get, hence fleet number 100 receiving a more random licence plate. The Leicester and Northampton fleets were numbered into a common series from 9 April 2000 and this vehicle then became 210.

East Lancs-bodied Volvo B10M 115 (J115 MRP), at Links View terminus, operates cross-town route 28 on 23 May 2000, covering for one of the two Mercedes minibuses normally used at that time. Part of the turning circle can be seen to the left of the picture. This was added in 1985 to eliminate reversing movements and allow the last of the crew-operated vehicles to be withdrawn.

Once pride of the coach fleet and numbered 1, D101 XNV was known as 211 by 13 August 2003, but also carried number 101. It is now downgraded with bus seats and operating route 3 from Hopping Hill, the estate now referred to as Ryehill. The red tarmaced kerb build-out was added to the bus stop in 1995, when this area was served by the first low-floor vehicles for the town.

Returning to Northampton from service in Leicester, where it had been since 1997, was 282 (LSU 717, F87 DVV) originally numbered 87. It retained original coach seats both upstairs and down. On 26 June 2000, a matter of days after returning home, the vehicle is about to operate the slow route 8 towards the town centre. This stop is Cranford Road and 'Kingsthorpe front' seen behind the bus has been completely redeveloped. The registration was previously carried on Leyland Leopard number 28.

Parklands Lower School on Spinney Hill Road is the location of 290 (H290 VRP). It still wears its local name scroll and First Northampton names on 24 December 2001 while operating route 11, which served Kettering Road. Someone had forgotten to peel off the 'o' from the roof dome when the bus was renumbered from 90! Compare other livery and lettering detail differences with the image on page 13.

Volvo Citybus 299 (J299 GNV), new as 99, loads for the town centre at Standens Barn Road on 21 April 2001, the last day of route 69. Local name *Charles Bradlaugh 1833–91* is still carried. An outspoken and rebellious MP for Northampton, his statue stands at Abington Square in the town centre, which 299 would have circled on its outbound journey.

Now delocalised, the same vehicle is seen at Links View terminus on 17 July 2002 simply carrying 'First' lettering. No superstitions exist at Northampton as this route regained its old number 13 in the April 2002 route changes.

Another Dennis from Leicester which Northamptonians got to know was the Falcon with smart Northern Counties bodywork. Six were operated, 620 (K620 SBC) being the first, pictured standing in on premium low-floor route 2 at Blackthorn Middle School on 1 July 2002.

Works buses and industrial services

Route 23 was a long-established route between the town centre and Brackmills Industrial Estate. Running AM & PM peaks only, the vehicles used on the service would operate other peak services or school work around them. With eighty-two seats the Volvo Citybuses were good crowd-shifters. 292 (H292 VRP) is seen at Kilvey Road about to commence an evening journey towards the town centre on 21 June 2002. The aroma of spices from the nearby British Pepper & Spice factory filled the air here.

Providing limited additional journeys to Brackmills off-peak was route 93. Two long-wheelbase Bristol VRs new to Lincoln City Transport were acquired in 1997, originally taking fleet numbers 46 and 47, which preceded native NT examples. Here 47 (UFW 41W) leaves the gloom of Greyfriars for Brackmills on 24 October 1997. With their services in Northampton complete both the twenty-two-year-old VRs headed for Western National in August 2002.

With many businesses relocating from the town centre to out-of-town business and industrial parks, the lunchtime shuttle services brought much needed custom back to the centre of Northampton. The 57 was jointly operated with Stagecoach and ran from Pavilion Drive in Brackmills to St Giles Street post office. Before a purpose-built bus stand was constructed here in October 2000 buses used stops along Pavilion Drive. Here 284 (F84 XBD), formerly 84, awaits more lunchtimers on 29 June 2000. This vehicle was the first to be fitted with dayglo blinds in late 1997.

Gas bus 45 (P502 MVV), new as 502, works unusual service 17 from Brackmills to Kingsthorpe via a very circuitous route and is seen on the A45 slip road about to turn into Pavilion Drive. The Keep public house is no more and the route was usually worked by double-deckers before and after school journeys. 25 February 2003 was within the school holidays and allowed for a more unusual vehicle on the route. The service was withdrawn on 21 November 2003.

A useful all-day service commencing 23 April 2001 was route 10. This ran from the railway station to Brackmills via the bus station, town centre and general hospital. The half-hourly service was initially worked by all vehicle types and here Alexander Dash-bodied Volvo B6 426 (L103 PWR) stands time at the railway station on 2 January 2001. New to Yorkshire Rider in 1994, the vehicle had also seen service with Eastern Counties and Leicester before arriving at Northampton.

At the same location MCW Metrobus 34 (AUT 34Y) works the service on 21 December 2001. Prior to the route's introduction those wanting Brackmills off-peak had a lengthy walk from either Bedford Road or Queen Eleanor Roundabout. Within the new railway station layout, this area is now occupied by a taxi rank.

Filling another lunchtime need, due to office relocation, was contract route 63. This ran from Northants County Council offices at 'The Lakes' to St Giles Street post office for council employees only. 282 (LSU 717, *F87 DVV*) operates the service on 21 December 2001. Shoosmith & Harrison solicitors, in the building behind the bus, had their own shuttle numbered 64!

With no fares to collect, vehicles without ticket machines could be used and these were generally older school bus types as exemplified by ex-Aberdeen Leyland Atlantean (URS 324X). Numbered 324/344/544 during its two years at Northampton, two of these identities are displayed at once! 544 was correct at the time of the photo on 4 March 2003. Ironically, from 30 June 2003 funding cuts to their own service saw the route become commercial and fares were charged.

At the north of Northampton is Moulton Park, containing offices, factories, warehouses and even a sports arena. Nationwide is one such significant employer here and the main site of the university with student halls neighboured the estate. Route 9 served it during peak hours with odd off-peak journeys. Most ran to and from the town centre through Kingsthorpe, Semilong and St James. Smartly turned out Volvo Citybus 95 (J295 GNV) at Holly Lodge Drive makes its way back towards town on 21 February 2000.

On one of the odd off-peak route 9 workings on 3 March 2000, ex-Eastern National Duple Dominant-bodied Leyland Tiger 410 (EWR 653Y) waits to set off for the town centre. New to West Yorkshire PTE, the bus is at Brickyard Spinney Road, Moulton Park, where the stop is located on a roundabout. At this time, Country Lion Coaches also ran a couple of journeys on the route.

Sister 409 (EWR 651Y) is at Lower Farm Road, Moulton Park on 11 February 2000 about to work the long route 54 to the town centre via the Eastern District. With a total journey time of over an hour it would have been a luxury to have a vehicle with coach seats! The 'Bus Grant' doors were operated by a foot switch in the cab, a feature unfamiliar to Northampton drivers. The NBC logo of United Counties can just be seen on the bus stop flag.

The 25 was rerouted in 2002 to start and finish at the railway station and became the principal frequent service on behalf of the university. On 20 February 2003 299 (J299 GNV) is about to leave the railway station stop for Park Campus which was the main university site. The route also served the campus and halls at St Georges Avenue. New headlights have been fitted and window stickers added to the lower saloon, advertising FareSaver tickets.

The 96 ran year-round and was a long and infrequent route running from Park Campus via Moulton Park to the eastern district. Standing at the Park Campus on-site bus stop ready for the evening journey, 288 (F88 DVV) would see little custom on 23 July 2002 as this was during the university holiday period. This bus, along with sister vehicle 282, had three seats added to the lower saloon in place of the luggage rack to make them eighty-five seaters.

On short-term loan from Mainline's Doncaster Depot was 749 (N749 CKY) in exchange for East Lancs Pyoneer rebodied Volvo Citybus 122, which Mainline required for use on a contract. 749 proved popular with staff and passengers alike throughout its stay. It is seen at St Georges Avenue by the university Avenue Campus operating route 28 on 14 October 2000. Behind the bus is The Racecourse, a large recreation ground which once had a horse racing stand and was latterly more noted for the annual hot air balloon festival.

When the Cobblers relocated to the football stadium at Sixfields in October 1994 a match day bus service was provided numbered 100. This ran from the Abington area where the old ground was located (now the cricket ground) through several areas of the town to the new ground. On 29 April 2000 288 (F88 DVV) has returned to the depot during the match, awaiting the final whistle to collect the supporters. Incidentally, the match result that day was Northampton 1 – 0 Mansfield Town.

School buses

The pair of ex-Lincoln Bristol VRs were acquired for their large seating capacity, which was ideal for schools work, route 300 being one such example. 46 (UFW 40W) is seen running dead along Wellingborough Road to start the morning run at Ecton Brook on 15 February 2000. At this time these were the last two Bristol VRs in service, their schedules containing positioning journeys on other routes that were open to the public, and therefore ideal for enthusiasts!

At the other end of the route, at St Mary's School on the afternoon of 18 June 2002, is former Capital Citybus Northern Counties-bodied Dennis Dominator 141 (B102 WUW). Beginning life in London as H2 in 1984, 141 was part of the Alternative Vehicle Evaluation programme on route 170. However, the children about to board would know little of this vehicle's history; it's just the bus home!

Numerically the last Alexander RV-bodied Volvo Citybus delivered to Northampton Transport, 132 (K132 GNH) is seen waiting on Spinney Hill Road by Northampton School for Girls on 18 February 2000. The 3C was a lengthy route that also served Northampton School for Boys on its way to Hopping Hill, the 'C' suffix denoting a school journey in similar fashion to LT. One of the last vehicles to carry this livery scheme, 132, like others of the batch, saw further service in Glasgow.

The 93 was another lengthy school route again serving both girls' and boys' schools ending at East Hunsbury, a Stagecoach area of the town. Former Leicester East Lancs-bodied Dennis Dominator 149 (F149 MBC) would have provided a lively journey for the afternoon run. Here it is at journey's end, Butts Road on 4 March 2003.

Another Alexander-bodied vehicle of Scottish origin was Leyland Atlantean 330 (URS 330X), new to Grampian. Having worked Northampton Borough school route 88 the bus is returning to the depot along St James Road on 19 December 2001. The bus was initially preserved when withdrawn from Northampton.

Following the arrival of the Volvo B7L batch, which took numbers in the 3xx series, the remaining Atlanteans were renumbered. URS 330X became 540 and is about to operate school route 90 from Northampton School for Girls to Holly Lodge Drive on 19 June 2003. This was one of only two remaining Atlanteans at this time, both of which were withdrawn at the end of the 2003 academic year.

A ride on 353 would have been a luxury for those travelling on the 87 to Great Billing on 6 March 2003. The Wright Eclipse-bodied Volvo B7L was new as 716 (MV02 VCU) and turns on the playground at Northampton School for Girls.

Again at the girls' school, this time at the stop for route 92, is ex-GMPTE Northern Counties-bodied Leyland Atlantean 6479 (ANA 629Y), which kept its old Huddersfield fleet number at Northampton. One of two former North Western Dennis Dominators used at Northampton waits behind. 12 September 2002.

One of the original school contracts acquired in April 1996 was the 85 running from Litchborough to Campion School, Bugbrooke. A low bridge en route dictated the use of single-deckers and the original Duple 300-bodied Volvo B10M 111 (E111 NNV) waits to cross Watling Street (A5) at Fosters Booth on 3 September 1996. (David Pike)

Five Alexander-bodied Leyland Leopards were used by Northampton Transport including 21 (GSO 81V) on route 86 at Pattishall on 20 May 1996, again heading to Campion School. It was previously Midland Bluebird 452 but new in January 1980 as Alexander (Northern) NPE81. The school bus fleet was not originally intended to be used on local services but this changed very early on! (David Pike)

Another bus with Scottish heritage on route 86 was Alexander-bodied MCW Metrobus 268 (BLS 432Y), the route by then requiring the use of a double-decker. It is seen at the village of Kislingbury while running dead to St James Depot on 20 July 2000.

Transferred from Leicester were a pair of Plaxton Paramount-bodied Leyland Tigers. On 20 July 1998, loading at the village of West Haddon on route 76 to Guilsborough School, was 18 (BUT 18Y). (David Pike)

Volvo Citybus 124 (K124 URP) is seen at Kilsby Green on 7 June 2000 about to operate route 392 to Guilsborough School. This village borders Warwickshire and the large rail freight terminal DIRFT with close road links to the M1, M6 and A14.

NT won the tender for route 60 between Northampton and Guilsborough on 9 March 1987 and was still operating it when the photo of Volvo Citybus 281 (E41 OAH) was taken at Creaton on 13 June 2000. The NT bus stop flag dates from 1987, as does the bus, being new to Great Yarmouth Transport. Having just worked route 392 the vehicle is running dead to St James Depot. Still with original coach seats fitted and a 'willow leaf' applied to the sides of the experimental livery, 281 had a dot matrix blind while sister 280 had roller blinds.

Six routes (numbered 132–137) for schools in Wellingborough commenced in April 1996, all passing through the village of Earls Barton. 202 (FUT 183V) was one of a trio of Dennis Dominators to be transferred from Leicester and was captured on route 135 while running along The Ridge between Wellingborough and Great Doddington on the afternoon of 20 May 1996. Volvo Citybus 101 is in hot pursuit on route 133. (David Pike)

One of a pair of handsome Duple 340-bodied Leyland Tigers was 19 (PXI 8935, *E352 KSF*), acquired from SMT where it was 352 but new to Eastern Scottish as YL352 in October 1987. It is operating route 137 through the village of Mears Ashby on 20 May 1996. Looking more modern than some of the other school bus acquisitions, the pair were used in private hire publicity material and saw use on such work. (David Pike)

Volvo Citybus 92 (H292 VRP) waits at the dedicated school bus stop, the flag of which carries a First Northampton label, outside the Wrenn School, Doddington Road site in Wellingborough on 29 March 2000. The 133 was a straightforward run to Earls Barton.

After completing a run to Ecton Brook on route 69 Volvo Citybus 128 (K128 GNH) has run dead to The Pyghtle, Wellingborough and waits for students of Sir Christopher Hatton School on 6 June 2000. The 135 would also serve Wrenn School and terminate within the Northampton Borough at Ecton Brook (Botmead Road). The vehicle's name, *Grand Junction Canal*, is still being carried.

Beyond the borough

On loan from Leicester in May 1996 was Dominator 186 (FUT 186V), operating along Welford Road on route 60 towards Guilsborough. The number of newly acquired contracts in such a short space of time put pressure on vehicle availability and short-term hires were relatively common during this period. (David Pike)

Back with route 60, as mentioned earlier, and another 1987 NT bus stop flag is in evidence on Church Lane at the village of Spratton. Northern Counties-bodied Volvo B6 434 (L6 GML) is in very different surroundings to its original stamping ground at Gatwick Airport or with Capital Citybus, from where it was transferred. Non-school days such as 16 April 2003 saw the use of single-deckers on the route.

First Northampton journeys latterly continued on to Thornby and Welford but eventually the tender for route 60 was lost to Centrebus. Here, on the very last day of operation, 25 April 2003, former Capital Citybus Alexander Dash-bodied Volvo B6 435 (L672 RMD) starts off the day from Guilsborough School at 07.08. Ending without ceremony, notices in the windows bade farewell to the route.

In 1999 the long-established Midland Red link between Northampton and Rugby was split at the county boundary. The Rugby to West Haddon section was kept by Midland Red South, Crick to Northampton being tendered to First Northampton and numbered 207–210. The new arrangements didn't allow for connections to be made. On 27 May 2000 Duple Dominant-bodied Leyland Tiger 411 (A660 KUM), downgraded with bus seating, is at Crick Posthouse Hotel, the westerly terminus adjacent to junction 18 of the M1. Route 209 was a Saturday variant running via the Bringtons and Upper Harlestone.

The Duple-bodied Volvo B10M single-deckers were frequently used on the Crick services. On 24 December 1999 112 (G112 ENV) works the 09.08 208 service from Crick to Northampton and has just left the village of Yelvertoft. Three narrow bridges over the Grand Union Canal (Leicester Branch) would be crossed before reaching the next village, West Haddon.

Making an unusual appearance on the last Saturday 210 journey from Northampton on 27 May 2000 was gas bus 46 (P503 MVV), formally 503, caught on camera outside the Wheatsheaf in Crick village before returning dead to Northampton. Not known for their reliability, a sigh of relief was breathed when the bus made it back to St James Depot!

Crossing over by a few hundred yards from Northampton Borough into Daventry District, the area of Moulton Leys lies between Moulton village and Northampton. The 3A was a Sunday-only operation and Scania 363 (V363 CNH) waits at Manning Road before heading back to town on 14 July 2002. At the time this was the only Sunday route to serve Kettering Road. 363 would later become 65663 and be operated by Somerset & Avon before moving north to Glasgow and Edinburgh.

The batch of new Wright Eclipse-bodied Volvo B7Ls from Manchester included seven unbranded vehicles which were the recommended choice for drivers on Sundays. 352, originally 742, (MV02 VAY) was the first of these generic vehicles and is seen on a wet Sunday 29 December 2002 at Moulton Lane. Becoming 66325 in the national number series the vehicle would go on to work in Bristol then Leeds.

New operations in the new city

In 1999 Milton Keynes Council expanded their Christmas P&R operations to run from two sites all-day Monday to Saturday, 25 October to New Year's Eve. First Northampton were awarded the contract and used six former Capital Citybus Northern Counties-bodied Volvo B6s. On 4 November 1999 432 (L5 GML) & 435 (L888 AMY) have arrived at the MK Coachway car park, joining the third vehicle for route 100 (seen behind 432), all having run dead from Northampton. The cabin to the right was used by 24-hour site security.

Both travel and parking were provided free for the public in a bid to ease congestion in the city centre. New to Gatwick Motors, 432 (L5 GML) was one of a trio to retain additional luggage racks and seat only twenty-eight. It is waiting on Midsummer Boulevard on 29 October 1999 outside the new theatre and gallery which had still to be opened. 432 went on to work in Leicester, Motherwell and, unusually after withdrawal from First, an independent operator in Birmingham, by then with a full forty-seat capacity.

Of similar type but originating with Capital Citybus was 431 (L888 JTC), seen leaving the Point bus stop H4 in the city centre for the Bowl on 26 October 1999. The Jetlink coach is en route to Gatwick and Brighton on the 747 which, at this time, had workings as far north as Milton Keynes. Most vehicles new to Capital Citybus in 1992 and 1993 had registrations containing '888', a numeral considered lucky by the Chinese who owned the company at the time. The initials of company senior officials were also included in the registrations.

433 (L281 RML) was another Volvo B6 new to First Capital, working route 100 to the Bowl. It is parked up on Silbury Boulevard by Milton Keynes library and council offices on 26 October 1999. The registration suffix letters are quite appropriate for an ex-London bus! In past years MK Metro had run a Saturdays-only P&R service to the Bowl.

The need for additional capacity on Saturdays at the Bowl site brought double-deckers from the main Northampton fleet. East Lancs-bodied Volvo Citybus 102 (D102 XNV) makes an unofficial stop in the winter sunshine at MK central bus station while running dead from Northampton on 4 December 1999. Still fitted with its original coach seats and only a two-track number blind, the correct route number 100 could not be displayed, so '10' would have to suffice! (A comparison can be made with the image on page 17)

At the Point bus stop H4 on Saturday 6 November 1999 both types of vehicle can be seen in use. From the main Northampton fleet is Citybus 123 (K123 URP), alongside the more usual P&R Volvo B6 431 (L888 JTC). Route 200 to the Coachway was not as established as the Bowl and the B6s could cope on the route on all six days.

Milton Keynes P&R work was won by Northampton in 2000 and 2001, but just to the Bowl site as MK Metro had begun a permanent year-round P&R service to MK Coachway in 2000. Ex-Capital Citybus Volvo B6s were the order of the day once again, this time bodied by Alexander. All were painted in First livery, which didn't wear well in wintry conditions! 438 (L680 RMD) waits at the Bowl on 18 December 2001. The bus shelter was relocated here from Elder Gate (adjacent to the railway station) in 1999.

Having established a low-floor fleet early on, this was used to Northampton's advantage on tendered work that specified the type. In October 2000 First won a tender for MK evening and Sunday route 1E between Newport Pagnell and the city centre, adding another operator to the mix in the area. Wright Axcess-Floline-bodied Scania L94 362 (V362 CNH) is seen near journey's end at Newport Pagnell Market Hill on 5 November 2000. First lost the contract on re-tender and the last day of operation was 19 November 2001.

Coaching and rail replacement duties

362 (V362 CNH) is away from its home town on Sunday 16 December 2001, working rail replacement duties on behalf of Midland Mainline at Kettering and about to operate the 12.30 departure to Market Harborough only. Becoming 65662, the vehicle would move firstly to work in the Bath area and latterly in East Scotland around Edinburgh.

With little Sunday work in Northampton a large group of buses and drivers was potentially available for rail replacement work or other duties. Former Bradford/Leeds Scania 365 (S101 CSG) is working Midland Mainline replacement work at Leicester with a service for Market Harborough and Kettering on 23 December 2001. Midland Railways architecture is again in evidence along with two traditional red telephone boxes.

Coach work continued throughout First ownership and a small rota of drivers worked private hire and contract work. The coaches would occasionally find their way onto schools and even local service work if required. 7 (N378 EAK), later reregistered NTL 655, is at Guilsborough School on 25 January 2000 operating route 314 to Great Oxendon. Rebuilt after an accident, the coach went on to be numbered 20055 and work in Somerset & Avon. The registration number was later transferred to an Alexander ALX400-bodied Volvo B7TL for University of Bath duties.

Plaxton Paramount 3500-bodied Volvo B10M 20037, formerly number 11, (SSU 837) has had rather untidy fleet numbers applied to its gold GRT coach-style livery. New to Yorkshire Rider as 1419 in 1990, with Gold Rider coach lettering, the vehicle has carried the registrations G73 RGG, 8995 WY and G427 PWW during its lifetime. Seen in Duston on 18 July 2004 it is about to take a group to Brighton for the day. Registration number SSU 837 is now owned by Tamworth Bus & Coach.

Coach and private hire operations have always featured at Northampton. At one time almost every vehicle had a calibrated tachograph fitted. Some, such as the four Duple 300-bodied Volvo B10Ms, were bought with service and coach work in mind. Last of the batch, 114 (G114 ENV), at St James Depot in July 1993, shows the final livery carried by these vehicles under council ownership. (Nigel Wheeler)

Optare Prisma-bodied Mercedes 0405N 502 (M502 GRY) was, on occasion, hired from Leicester as it was fitted with a tachograph. Wearing the GRT 'advance' livery, it is taking a break at Upton roundabout on 14 June 2000 before heading back to Leicester, after use on a hire the previous day.

The coaches too were shared between Northampton and Leicester. 20418 (P176 NAK) was numbered 2 at Leicester and was one of a matching pair of Volvo B10Ms with Plaxton Premiere bodies acquired from dealer stock when only a couple of years old. Both were transferred to First Hampshire and Dorset for use principally as training vehicles and were still performing this role in 2016. Seen at the Provincial Society rally at Stokes Bay on 7 August 2011.

Super low-floor and not-so-super gas buses

Northampton Transport was one of the first twenty operators in the UK to introduce low-floor vehicles in October 1995. These were Volvo B10L chassis with Alexander Ultra bodywork to the design of Swedish manufacturer Saffle. By then owned by GRT, company officials and guests attend a launch event beside one of the trio at Hopping Hill turning circle, served by route 28, which would benefit from the new type of bus. (St Giles Photography/author's collection)

Seen when only a few months old is 43 (N43 RRP), photographed on Weggs Farm Road, St Giles Park, on its regular 27 route in the summer of 1996. The original Northampton Transport lettering on the sides has already been replaced and the First Bus 'f' logo added. The Wayfarer II ticket machine can clearly be seen, the company upgrading to the mark 3 version in July 1997. Climate control was specified on the trio although in the warmer months of the year the saloon and cab would become unpleasantly hot. Opening windows were eventually fitted. (David Pike)

Volvo B10L 41 (N41 RRP) stands on Berrywood Road, Duston on 15 August 2002 before taking up duty on route 27. The blind was set for the photograph to show 'Greyfriars Bus Station', the subject of proposed demolition even then. Note the two-piece windscreen that was fitted at the same time the interior was refurbished to First Group standard. The trio were transferred to Manchester later that year to join similar examples originating with Timeline and South Wales Transport (the latter were all ex-demonstration vehicles). This bus became 591 and later 61242 in the initial national renumbering scheme. Ironically most of the Manchester B10Ls would be transferred to Northampton in 2004, the NT examples included!

On 26 June 1997 a press launch with Glenda Jackson (then Minister for Transport) took place for the gas bus fleet. The six vehicles were again Volvo B10L chassis with Alexander Ultra bodywork. Cross-town routes 29/79 were designed for the buses and linked Kingsthorpe with Ecton Brook via the town centre. The public launch day was 30 June 1997 and free travel was available at the Kingsthorpe end of the route. 502 (P502 MVV) loads at the library stop.

Free travel awaits those who board 504 (P504 MVV) on launch day, 30 June 1997, at the route's terminus, Welford Road layby, opposite the North Star pub. The gas 'pod' can be seen on the roof over the first and second window bays. Red bus stops were a feature of the routes, as were the 'red carpets' of bricks or tarmac and 'Kassel' kerbing. The names of the partners involved in the gas bus scheme are displayed on each of the main side windows.

Quality corridors with low-floors

Described in publicity as 'Super low floor' vehicles, in 1997 Northampton received three Wright Axcess-Ultralow-bodied Scania L113s numbered 341–3. These were from a batch of six shared with Leicester, where they were registered. Originally used on routes 2 and 10 to Kings Heath, they would also work other quality routes such as the 27. 343 (R343 SUT) is seen at the top of Bridge Street on 27 May 1999. The bus went on to work in Glasgow numbered 61563, after a very brief spell with Eastern Counties. This type would be the last to be used by Northampton, as readers will see later on.

The next batch of three similar vehicles arriving in Northampton also carried Leicester registrations and had Scania L94 chassis. However, the bodywork was now marketed as Axcess-Floline. On 20 May 2000 361 (S361 MFP), numerically the last, is seen here at Weggs Farm Road, St Giles Park, the westerly terminus of route 27 for which the bus is branded. The destination display was now programmed to alternate between terminus and via points.

Following a fire in August 1999 at Abbey Park Road Depot in Leicester the three R-registered Scanias were transferred there. Some DAF vehicles were hired pending delivery of three replacement Scanias, which carried on the sequence 362–4. The trio were registered in Northampton, the last to be done so under the old-style registration system. When only a couple of weeks old on 22 December 1999, 363 (V363 CNH) is at Ladybridge Drive, Shefleys.

Sister vehicle 364 (V364 CNH) is seen at Hunsbury Hill Road, West Hunsbury on 26 July 2000. Good bus stop publicity featured on route 27. These vehicles went on to work for First Badgerline at Bath and ended their days in Edinburgh with national fleet numbers 65662–4.

The original gas bus routes were changed just over a year after they were launched. They settled on routes 29/30, which again were cross-town and linked Kingsthorpe (Acre Lane) to Kings Heath. First of the batch, 501 (P501 MVV) is seen at Welford Road 'North Star' terminus on 21 February 2000. The bus would carry on to make the loop of Acre Lane, which a similar vehicle seen in the distance has already completed. The lettering on the front still states 'Brought to you by FirstBus' some two years after the plc was retitled 'First Group'. The bus became 44 in 2000 and national number 66001 in 2004.

Off its branded route, Scania 361 (S361 MFP) is seen at the Kings Heath terminus on 27 February 1999 with original nearside mirror arm still fitted. The bus would transfer to Bolton in 2002 and become 61141.

Also at Kings Heath, this time South Oval, on 18 July 2000 is Scania L94 367 (S104 CSG), about to make its way around the loop. These group standard buses were only eighteen months old when they arrived at Northampton from Bradford. However, the bus was new to Leeds Bramley Garage as 8104. Moving on again in 2002 to Queens Road Depot in Manchester, the bus was given a new identity – 61139.

Soon after arriving at Northampton the majority of the Wright Eclipse-bodied Volvo B7Ls received 'Overground' brand names and colour-coded route branding. This was applied in a style First Group used nationally at the time. 347 (MV02 VCT), new as 715, is a 'purple line' bus for routes 29/30 and is seen at Welford Road terminus on 30 December 2002.

Needs must and sometimes step-entrance vehicles appeared on the quality routes or those intended for low-floor operation. At the St Giles Park shops, Weggs Farm Road terminus of route 27 is former Leicester Dennis Falcon 623 (L623 XFP) with Northern Counties Paladin bodywork. The picture was taken on 23 June 2003.

Cross-town route 3 was the 'yellow line' although no vehicles were branded and any type could operate on the route. On 14 January 2003 gas bus 47 (P504 MVV), new as 504 and latterly 66004, is seen at the Hopping Hill terminus where Northampton's low-floor buses were launched some eight years earlier (see the image on page 67). The dot matrix number blind was stuck on '33', the right digit at least! The main destination was a driver-operated roller blind. None of the gas bus batch would reach their tenth anniversary, all being scrapped in late 2006.

Settling on 'red line' route 2 was Volvo B7L 338 (MV02 VCW), new as 717 and later numbered 66343, seen at the Blackthorn Middle School stop while operating the loop around Rectory Farm on 21 January 2003.

Still wearing its Manchester fleet number 771, MV02 VDA (later 339 and lastly 66347) is running dead along Wellingborough Road on 21 September 2002 to take up service on route 2 at Rectory Farm. First Northampton didn't operate along this major road at the time. The destination blind scrolled to read 'First Northampton, bringing you low-floor, easy access buses!!!' One of the batch to be exchanged with Norwich and replaced by older Scanias in 2012, the bus would move on again to Bradford and was still in service late in 2019.

Minibuses, playing a small role

In 1987 Northampton Transport tried a batch of eight Alexander-bodied Renault Dodge S56s. Numerically the last, 110 (E110 JNH) is seen at St James Depot in July 1993. Despite the appealing twenty-three coach seats and each taking a girl's name (in this case *June*) the batch were unpopular with passengers and staff from the off. Every effort was made to dispose of the batch and even at the time of the picture only four remained. When GRT took the company over these would transfer to Aberdeen. (Nigel Wheeler)

Just over a decade later, in 1998 the Renault Dodge minibus would again appear in Northampton with a batch arriving from First Centrewest carrying Wright bodywork. History repeated itself with the buses proving very unpopular. Leicester also received the type in larger numbers and after withdrawal some were stored at Northampton pending their fate. These were 704/705/792 (HDZ 5479/77/67). Compare the rough surface of the yard, which still shows the outlines of former buildings, to that in the image on page 21.

More popular were a pair of Marshall-bodied Mercedes Benz Vario 0814Ds, which again were acquired from First Centrewest where they were used in Uxbridge. At this time the Links View route (formally the 13) had been joined with the 28 to Hopping Hill. This was the regular haunt of the pair and 720 (P826 NAV) is at Links View on 9 December 1999. Formerly numbered MM26 at Uxbridge, it just made the national renumbering and became 51826.

Both Varios retained their old livery for some time, bringing red buses back to Northampton on a small scale! Seen on Marefair on 30 September 2000, 720 (P826 MAV) has by now had an electronic number blind added, a reused side screen from a withdrawn Renault Dodge.

The pair of Marshall-bodied Mercedes Benz Varios were eventually repainted into full 'FG2' livery, as displayed by 720 (P826 MAV) on 15 December 2001 at MK Bowl. MK P&R drivers had a 'travelling bus' for crew changes mid-afternoon. Later in their lives at Northampton the Varios would be branded for Monday to Friday route 10 and saw use on the Saturdays-only Banbury contract routes.

No type of vehicle was exempt from Northampton! Numbered 912 in the ancillary fleet, Ford Transit C930 GYD was new to Southern National as 368 in 1986 and used by Leicester as a staff bus since 2000. On loan to Northampton during late 2001 it is seen on 18 December at the Bowl in Milton Keynes as the 'travelling bus', due to depart at 17.10 and take early shift drivers back to Northampton. Unusually it was repainted into the green and yellow experimental livery. With makeshift blinds it is unlikely the bus ever made it into revenue-earning service!

On loan

When the trio of original Wright-bodied Scanias was sent to Leicester in August 1999 three DAFs were hired pending arrival of replacements. One was bodied by Ikarus, the other two by Northern Counties and had previously been used at Gatwick Airport. Numbered 803 for its stay, P905 PWW was operating MK P&R route 100 on 27 October 1999, contrary to the destination blinds!

To help with vehicle availability during 2002 several Optare Prisma-bodied Mercedes Benz 0405Ns were borrowed from Leicester. These smart vehicles were popular with drivers and the public and worked over a number of routes. New in 1995, the batch of ten were purchased during the GRT era. 501 (M501 GRY) in 'FG 2' livery is at Crick Holiday Inn, formerly the Posthouse hotel, on 3 July 2002 about to work route 207 to Northampton with little need that day for the tinted windows.

Mainline's Doncaster depot had loaned 749 (N749 CKY), a Volvo B10M with Alexander PS bodywork, in exchange for Northmpton's Volvo Citybus 122 (WSU 481, K122 URP) which was required for a contract. Here it is on 7 October 2000 at St James Depot after completing a Saturday morning working on route 20. The red walkway was the designated path between the offices, the fuel alley and workshop area.

Fleet movements were substantial in 2002. Pending the arrival of the Wright-bodied Volvo B7Ls, due from Manchester after their use on Commonwealth Games duties, a batch of Volvo B10BLEs with Wright Renown bodies were hired from Mainline. Northampton's own similar Scania vehicles were away for rectification work pending their eventual withdrawal. First of the batch was 781 (R781 WKW), seen at Rectory Farm Road on 22 July 2002.

At Mereway Tesco on 27 July 2002, operating route 27 which at this time was curtailed to terminate at this point, is 783 (R783 WKW). The 'R' registered vehicles had interiors to a pre-First Mainline standard with red seat fabric and yellow handrails. Most ran without destination blinds during their stay.

Last of the 'R' registered batch was 790 (R790 WKW) operating on route 29 around the Acre Lane loop on 8 August 2002. The window stickers were adverts in the shape of thought bubbles for Mainline routes and fare offers and a Northampton destination blind was fitted. Returning to Sheffield by October 2002 and later becoming 60627, the bus finished its service life at Rotherham as late as 2015 and is now preserved by the South Yorkshire Transport Trust.

Three members of the 'S' registered batch, which were to full First Group specification, were also used. Interestingly their destination blinds were the opposite way around to the previous batch. 791 (S791 RWG) is operating route 2 at Blackthorn Middle School on 3 August 2002. Several members of this batch moved to Hampshire after their loan and this vehicle would eventually become number 66191.

A little different were a pair of Leyland Lynxes from Worcester. 1136/1137 (G136/7 HNP) were used in July and August 2003, settling on running numbers 39 and 42 for route 4/4A. 1137 is seen on Chalcombe Avenue on the 4A on 11 July 2003. From early 2004 Leicester would acquire members of this batch, including 1136, to operate services there. This vehicle, however, would become a driver trainer with West Yorkshire carrying national number 62737 and was eventually scrapped in August 2007.

Seasonal events and the 1998 flood

Northampton had previously used Lynxes in April 1998 when two were loaned from Bristol. This was immediately after the once-in-a-lifetime floods experienced over the Easter weekend that caused extensive flooding to areas near the River Nene. This included St James, and the depot had a 'high tide' of about 3 feet! 1653 (H653 YHT) of Lawrence Hill Depot is seen on 11 April 1998 at the temporary facilities set up in the car park of Northampton Town Football Club's Sixfields stadium.

Vehicles were borrowed from six operators within First, bringing many different liveries and vehicle types for a three-day period. From Eastern National came ECW-bodied Leyland Olympian 4021 (C421 HJN) with coach seats on route 29 heading towards Ecton Brook from Greyfriars bus station. It is 11 April 1998, and Colchester's Hippodrome gets its money's worth out of its side advert!

The furthest north vehicles were borrowed from was Leeds, who sent these smart Northern Counties-bodied Scania L113 double-deckers. The response to hiring vehicles at such short notice was commendably rapid. At Greyfriars bay H the driver of 8010 (H810 TWX) can set the numbers at least for route 20 to Southfields on 11 April 1998, but would have to continue using emergency tickets for the day.

Coming from closer to home were Dennis Dominators from Leicester. Externally these had the same livery as Northampton and 72 (A72 FRY) departs Greyfriars bus station on route 25 towards Kingsthorpe. Some vehicles such as those from Leicester stayed longer or were rehired, as Northampton's fleet received mechanical attention. This view was taken on 16 September 1998.

Almost a year to the day since the floods, April 1999 saw a vandal attack on St James Depot targeting mainly windscreens, which put most of the fleet out of action. As well as First Group companies loaning vehicles some were from other sources, in this case Confidence of Leicester 24 (HOR 306N), new to Portsmouth Corporation. Keeping a naval theme, this Alexander-bodied Leyland Atlantean wears a battleship-inspired livery. Resting between duties on route 22 at Greyfriars on 2 April 1999, this vehicle is now preserved. (David Henderson)

The annual Balloon Festival was a significant event in the town's calendar. This was held on The Racecourse (which we saw on page 46) and attracted large crowds. P&R operations ran throughout the weekend from three sites and vehicles were hired from fellow company Leicester. East Lancs-bodied Dennis Dominator 152 (F152 MBC) waits on Trinity Avenue, where the bus stop was segregated from other traffic. Operating route C to the University Park Campus on 18 August 2000, this bus was no stranger to Northampton, having been part of the fleet in 1997 numbered 204.

Leicester had recently acquired a number of Alexander-bodied Volvo Olympians from Glasgow, one of which was 188 (P188 TGD) still in its previous operator's livery – simply red! It is operating P&R route S from Sixfields Stadium at Walter Tull Way bus stop on 18 August 2000. All three routes were jointly operated with Stagecoach. After use at Leicester the bus went on to work in Essex, Worcester and Stoke-on-Trent, carrying national number 34288.

There are nearly double the number of traffic lights than buses in this view on Weedon Road, but for first thing on a Sunday morning that was still a lot of buses. It is 7 July 2002 and almost every vehicle in the depot headed to Hinton Airfield near Brackley to work a P&R route to Silverstone racing circuit for the Formula One event. The job was sub-contracted from Stagecoach and it transpired none of these additional vehicles would be required.

Significant network changes, 2001 and 2002

Major changes were introduced to the route network from Sunday 23 April 2001. One of the affected routes that would cease was the 20, and here 282 (LSU 717, F87 DVV) operates along Billing Road East two days earlier. New route 5 would use Weston Mill Lane to the left of the picture and serve Riverside Retail Park via a bus gate.

The 79 route variant is depicted by Volvo Citybus 128 (K128 GNH) operating along Bridgewater Drive in Abington Vale on 21 April 2001, the last day of the route's operation. The livery looks plain without the magenta 'fade out' band. Becoming 38128 in the national fleet number series, the bus would head to Bolton for further service, along with sister 127.

Also operating along Bridgewater Drive, but in the outbound direction, on 1 March 2002 is Volvo Citybus 122 (WSU 481, *K122 URP*) with 1998 East Lancs Pyoneer rebody. Unfortunately the destination of '5A Ecton Brook' could not be shown on the dot matrix blinds so hand-drawn sheets are the order of the day.

Sister vehicle 123 (K123 URP), which still carries its original Alexander RV bodywork, operates long-established cross-town route 26. On 21 April 2001, the driver is about to set down on Hunsbury Hill Road, the penultimate stop before the Camp Hill terminus at the southern end of the route. The bus would then return north to Kingsthorpe. The new routes were to be the 5/5A linking this area to the east of Northampton, as we have seen earlier.

April 2002 saw long-established circular routes 4 and 5 become the 4 and 4A, joined up to former Kingsthorpe route 26. On 26 July 2003 Volvo Citybus 284 (F84 XBD) works along Headlands at the former terminus of route 5. On the upper deck, bus seats have replaced the ECW-type dual-purpose seating (compare to the image on page 30). A member of the original batch of Citybuses, this vehicle would carry on in service with First Edinburgh as 38084, past its twentieth birthday.

Snaking its way around Hunsbarrow Road, Briar Hill is 128 (K128 GNH), working a 5A from Ecton Brook to Camp Hill on 2 August 2003.

The Shelfleys and West Hunsbury areas on quality route 27 were withdrawn completely from the April 2002 changes, the route being curtailed at Mereway Tesco. Following complaints from residents, a council-funded hourly route 50 commenced on 24 June 2002, until the service was joined back up to the 27 in September of the same year. Any type could work the route and here gas bus 44 (P501 MVV) is seen at West Hunsbury on 19 August 2002. The bus shelter was one of several of these green painted structures introduced around the town around 1992, and made of recycled materials.

When the 2004/5 deliveries of single- and double-deck Volvo B7s began, many of the Alexander-bodied Volvo Citybuses were transferred to depots in Edinburgh and Glasgow. Their appearance, both internally and externally, was greatly improved and here former Northampton 129 (K129 GNH), now 38129, on Glasgow's 'Gold star' route X3 is about to enter Buchanan bus station. It is a long way from the Market Square after which the bus was once named. Many of the former Northampton Citybuses saw more than twenty years of service. (Author's collection)

Other vehicles to head north were the pair of former Great Yarmouth East Lancs-bodied Volvo Citybuses. Its appearance now more corporate, E40 OAH, numbered 1198 with Lowland, is seen at the Metrocentre bus rally in May 2002. One of Northampton's original pair of 1986 East Lancs Volvos also joined Lowland. Their original interior condition can be seen on page 15. (Author's collection)

The final chapter begins

Nine of these smart Wright Eclipse Gemini-bodied Volvo B7TLs were delivered in 2005. These were the first new double-deckers at Northampton since the 1993 Volvo Citybus batch 127–32. 32632 (KP54 KBJ) on route 30 heads along Gladstone Road, Spencer Estate towards Kings Heath on 22 August 2005. After only a year just two of this batch would remain in Northampton (32629/30) almost until the close of the depot. 32632 went on to work in Leicester and Stoke-on-Trent. (David Pike)

Numerically the first of ten Wright Eclipse-bodied Volvo B7RLEs, 66962 (KX05 MHY) would be the sole survivor, lasting in Northampton until late 2007. These vehicles were visually similar to the twenty-five Volvo B7Ls received in 2002 but with orange LED destination equipment and the tidier underfloor engine arrangement making for a more logical interior. The bus is on Abington Street on 27 October 2007 as part of a NFBU surgery inviting comments and suggestions from the travelling public of Northampton. (Raymond Bedford)

With ten single-deck Wright Eclipse-bodied Volvo B7RLEs also being delivered to Northampton in 2005, the fleet was looking impressive. Sadly this wouldn't last as just over a year after their entry into service, just over half of these new single- and double-deck vehicles had transferred to other depots within the Midlands division. More would follow, including 66968 (KX05 MJO), caught on camera on 8 May 2008 at St Margaret's bus station in its new home city of Leicester.

A number of the Alexander RV-bodied Volvo Citybuses went to and fro between Northampton, Redditch and Worcester. Some were repainted for use on 'Green Bus' contract work like 38124 (K124 URP), which leads the line-up at Redditch Depot on 16 June 2008. When this depot was sold to Diamond Bus three of the type were inherited and used by them, with former 126 (K126 URP) lasting until August 2015.

The Dennis Lance with Plaxton Verde body was the main type to replace the newer stock. Most were new to Midland Red West like 67203 (L203 AAB), seen here on 24 June 2008 in Drapery operating route 5 from Southfields. One of the 'MV02' batch of Volvo B7Ls follows behind. This chassis and body combination was favoured by the Badgerline Group and appeared across a number of the constituent fleets.

The type were also regular performers on routes 207 and 208, by now sensibly running right through to Rugby as in Stagecoach Midland Red days. 67204 (L204 AAB) is seen at North Street, Rugby on 8 May 2008 heading for home. After First's era ended, the services would return to Stagecoach once more and would be renumbered to the more traditional 96.

The penultimate route to be operated by First Northampton was the 4A to Kingsthorpe, Acre Lane where we once saw gas buses. Operating the service on 16 October 2012 was Dennis Lance 67237 (L237 AAB) at Langham Place near the cathedral. This bus was sold from Northampton service to preservation in July 2013. One of the former First Eastern Counties Wright-bodied Scanias pulls in behind. (David Henderson)

The final route to be operated was the 2 running between the town centre and Rectory Farm, unchanged since introduction on 23 April 2001. The majority of the 2002 Wright Eclipse-bodied Volvo B7Ls were exchanged with First Eastern Counties for more elderly Wright Axcess-Ultralow-bodied Scania L113s. Most were in a poor state externally but were actually good solid vehicles. Northampton had used three such vehicles of the same vintage but from new, back in 1997. 65580 (T580 JNG) operates along Kettering Road at Eastern Park Parade on 16 October 2012. (David Henderson)

Unusually, the operation of a shuttle service on behalf of First Capital Connect, between Luton Airport and Luton Parkway railway station, was run by Northampton from an outstation at Eaton Green Road, Luton. This passed to First Essex at Chelmsford when Northampton closed. Here articulated Mercedes Benz Citaro 10033 (T3 FCC, KR52 ZSV, 02 D 74688) is at Luton Airport on 11 September 2009. New to First's Aircoach operation at Dublin Airport, three of this type were used at Luton. (Raymond Bedford)

The 'Ftr' is here! – 'future', in non-text speak. The concept was trialled in Leeds and Swansea and gave a tram feel to the bus operation. These smart articulated Wright-bodied Volvo B7LAs were prematurely withdrawn from both cities with some going on to work at other First depots. 19031 (YJ07 LVX), originally from Leeds, is also at Luton Airport on 11 September 2009. It was later reregistered T6 FCC. (Raymond Bedford)

The end is nigh. Scania 65563 (R263 DVF) is about to begin the final journey operated by First Northampton on route 2 from Rectory Farm towards town. The time is 20.28 on the last day of service, Saturday 14 September 2013. (David Henderson)

Passengers were allowed to travel with 65563 from Greyfriars bus station to St James Depot to mark the significant event. With the journey complete the fueller/ shunter is about to close the door on a total of 132 years' service by Northampton Transport to the public of the county town. (David Henderson)

We end with some old red buses! The opportunity to take a tour and have one last look around St James Depot arose on Saturday 5 May 2014. This was some eight months after the official closure and the sound of diesel engines echoed off the walls one last time. These three Daimlers (246/267/154) are all preserved. The land and property were sold to Church's shoes, whose factory sits adjacent to the site. The intention is to expand their operations into this building, but at the time of writing this had not yet commenced.